Note to parents, carers and teachers

Read it yourself is a series of modern stories, favourite characters, traditional tales and first reference books, written in a simple way for children who are learning to read. The books can be read independently or as part of a guided reading session.

Each book is carefully structured to include many high-frequency words vital for first reading. The sentences on each page are supported closely by pictures to help with understanding, and to offer lively details to talk about.

The books are graded into four levels that progressively introduce wider vocabulary and longer text as a reader's ability and confidence grows.

Ideas for use

- Although your child will now be progressing towards silent, independent reading, let her know that your help and encouragement is always available.

- Developing readers can be concentrating so hard on the words that they sometimes don't fully grasp the meaning of what they're reading. Answering the quiz questions at the end of the book will help with understanding.

For more information and advice on Read it yourself and book banding, visit **www.ladybird.com/readityourself**

Book Band 9

Level 4 is ideal for children who are ready to read longer stories with a wider vocabulary and are eager to start reading independently.

Special features:

Richer, more varied vocabulary

Full exploration of subject

Detailed illustrations capture the imagination

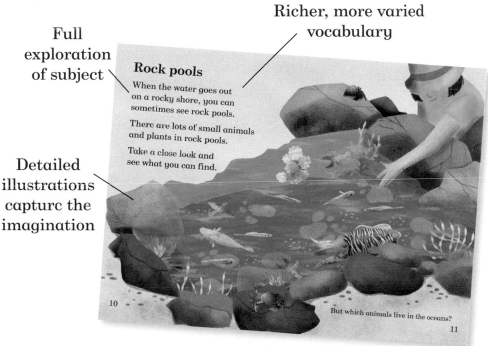

Rock pools

When the water goes out on a rocky shore, you can sometimes see rock pools.

There are lots of small animals and plants in rock pools.

Take a close look and see what you can find.

10

But which animals live in the oceans?

11

Longer sentences

Captions offer further explanation

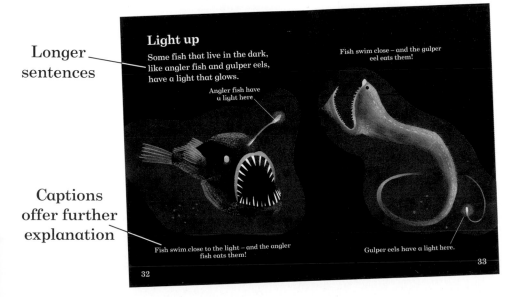

Light up

Some fish that live in the dark, like angler fish and gulper eels, have a light that glows.

Angler fish have a light here

Fish swim close – and the gulper eel eats them!

Fish swim close to the light – and the angler fish eats them!

Gulper eels have a light here.

32

33

Educational Consultant: Geraldine Taylor
Book Banding Consultant: Kate Ruttle
Subject Consultant: Steve Parker

LADYBIRD BOOKS

UK | USA | Canada | Ireland | Australia
India | New Zealand | South Africa

Ladybird Books is part of the Penguin Random House group of companies
whose addresses can be found at global.penguinrandomhouse.com.

www.penguin.co.uk   www.puffin.co.uk   www.ladybird.co.uk

Penguin
Random House
UK

First published 2017
This edition 2019
002

Copyright © Ladybird Books Ltd, 2017

Printed in China

A CIP catalogue record for this book is available from the British Library

ISBN: 978–0–241–40540–6

All correspondence to:
Ladybird Books
Penguin Random House Children's
One Embassy Gardens, 8 Viaduct Gardens, London SW11 7BW

In the Ocean

Written by Zoë Clarke

Illustrated by Stephanie Fizer Coleman

Contents

Amazing world

The world is amazing and most of it is water!

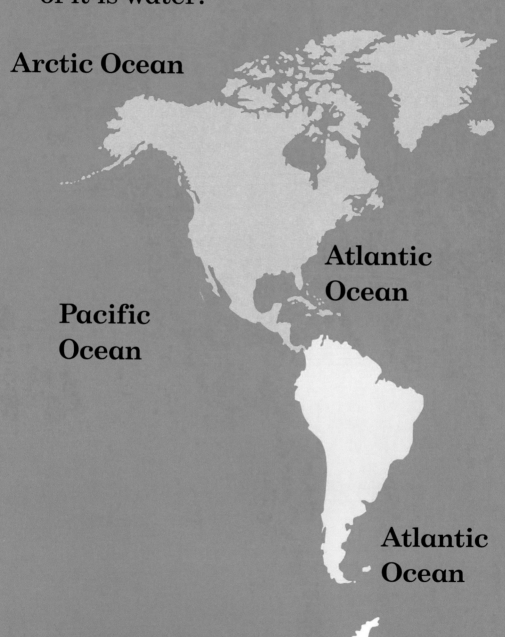

Arctic Ocean

Atlantic Ocean

Pacific Ocean

Atlantic Ocean

Here are the oceans. Many animals in the world live in the oceans.

Pacific Ocean

Indian Ocean

Southern Ocean

Rock pools

When the water goes out
on a rocky shore, you can
sometimes see rock pools.

There are lots of small animals
and plants in rock pools.

Take a close look and
see what you can find.

But which animals live in the oceans?

Coral reefs

You can find coral in water that is clean, not cold and not deep.

Coral is a rock made by lots and lots of coral animals.

A reef is made up of many different coral animals.

coral

Fish and other small animals live on coral reefs.

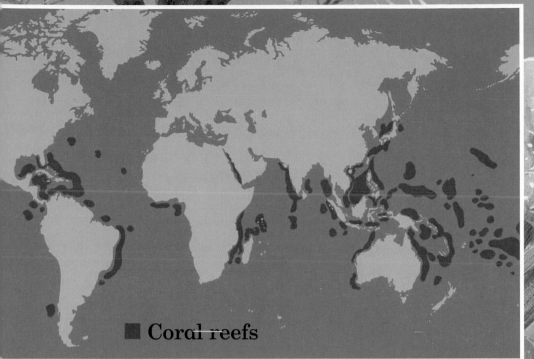

Coral reefs

There are coral reefs in the Atlantic,
Pacific and Indian Oceans.

13

Camouflage

Some animals that live on coral reefs look like plants, so that other animals do not eat them. This is called camouflage.

Some fish use camouflage to look like rocks. When other fish swim by, the camouflaged fish eats them in a flash!

Jellyfish

Swim away from the coral and you may see jellyfish.

Jellyfish live in all the oceans.

Some jellyfish can sting, too!

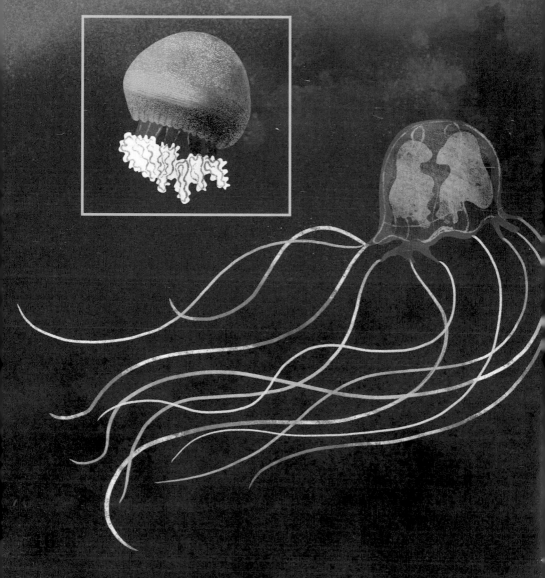

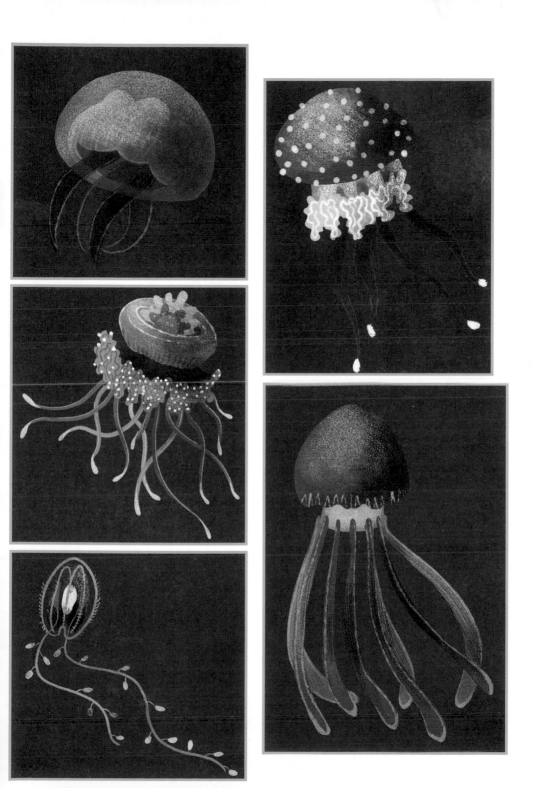

Jellyfish can be many different colours.

Spines and stings!

Many animals in the oceans have spines and stings.

Scorpion fish have very sharp spines! They use the spines to sting other animals.

scorpion fish

Stargazer fish have an electric sting.

stargazer fish

In a shell

Many animals in the oceans have shells to protect themselves.

The giant spider crab has a hard shell so it is hard to eat it.

Tiny animals live on the spider crab's shell.

Giant clams have big, hard shells, which are lots of different colours.

Lots of very tiny plants live in the clam.

Colour change

Some animals, like the blue-ringed octopus, flash different colours to warn other animals to go away.

The blue-ringed octopus is here.
Its colours flash a warning – go away!

The skin of this cuttlefish looks like it has many different colours at the same time.

Cuttlefish flash many different colours.

Giant squid!

The giant squid has long arms and two very long tentacles. The arms and tentacles catch other animals for the squid to eat.

Giant squid live in all of the world's oceans.

Giant squid have
the biggest eyes
in the world!

Sharp teeth

Most sharks have sharp teeth.
Do not go too close!

Some sharks eat small animals.
This shark eats big animals and
other sharks.

sharp teeth

Sharks can get very big, but they are not the biggest animals in the ocean.

hammerhead shark

mako shark

The biggest animal in the world

The blue whale is the biggest animal in the world.

Blue whales eat lots and lots of very tiny animals.

Deep down in the dark

Deep down in the ocean it is very dark and very cold.

The animals that live here like the cold, and they can live with no light.

Many of them look very different from other animals in the ocean!

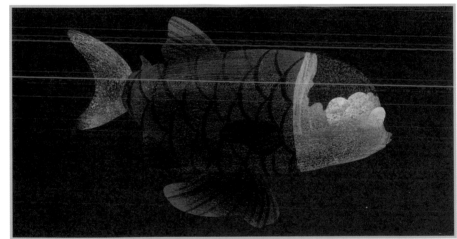

barreleye ↑

31

Light up

Some fish that live in the dark, like angler fish and gulper eels, have a light that glows.

Angler fish have a light here

Fish swim close to the light – and the angler fish eats them!

Fish swim close – and the gulper
eel eats them!

Gulper eels have a light here,

Finding new animals

New animals are being found in the oceans even now.

This is a ninja shark! It has very dark skin which may disguise it from other fish.

Its skin glows in the dark!

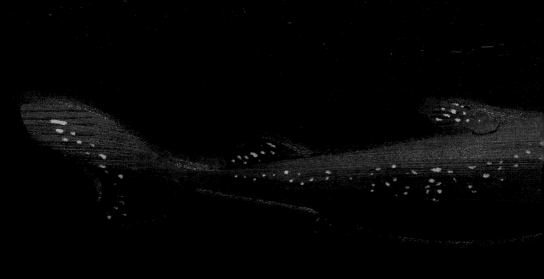

The ninja shark was found here, in the Pacific Ocean in 2015.

Ninja sharks
found here

The oceans in danger

Many animals and plants that live in the oceans are in danger.

People catch fish to eat, but if we catch too many, the fish may disappear.

We must protect our
oceans by not catching
too many fish!

Rubbish in the oceans

One of the biggest dangers to the oceans is rubbish, like plastic. Sea animals eat the rubbish and this harms them.

Plastic rubbish is even found in
the Southern and Arctic Oceans.

plastic

What can we do?

We can clean up the shore
and the oceans.

Collecting rubbish from the shore.

We could make a machine like this,
which could find rubbish, like plastic,
in the water.

The plastic is taken out of
the water.

Take care of the oceans

The oceans are amazing.

We must protect them from harm, or all the animals and plants in the oceans may disappear.

We have to care for, and clean up the oceans now.